CRAFTS
for
Accessorizing
that Look

written by
Susannah Blake

 Enslow Publishers, Inc.
40 Industrial Road
Box 398
Berkeley Heights, NJ 07922
USA
http://www.cnslow.com

This edition published by Enslow Publishers Inc.

Library of Congress Cataloging-in-Publication Data
Blake, Susannah.
Crafts for accessorizing that look /
Susannah Blake.
pages cm. -- (Eco chic)
Audience: 9-12
Audience: Grade 4 to Grade 6
Summary: "Create your own jewelry using
recycled materials"--Provided by publisher.
Includes bibliographical references.
ISBN 978-0-7660-4313-8
1. Handicrafts -- Juvenile literature. 2. Recyling [Waste, etc.]
3. Gifts -- Juvenile literature.
I. Title II. Series
TX 171.883 2013
745.5--dc23
2012025481
Cataloging-in-Publication Data available from the Library of Congress

Future editions:
Paperback ISBN: 978-1-4644-0571-6

Printed in China
122012 WKT, Shenzhen, Guangdong, China

10 9 8 7 6 5 4 3 2 1

First published in the UK in 2012 by Wayland
Copyright © Wayland 2012
Wayland
338 Euston Rd
London NW1 3BH

Editors: Julia Adams; Katie Woolley
Craft stylist: Annalees Lim
Designer: Rocket Design (East Anglia) Ltd
Photographer: Simon Pask, N1 Studios

Wayland is a division of Hachette Children's Books,
an Hachette UK company.
www.hachette.co.uk

Picture acknowledgements:
All step-by-step and craft photography:
Simon Pask, N1 Studios; images used throughout for creative
graphics: Shutterstock.com

*Fabulous fluffy
bangle
Page 14*

*Pretty pendant
Page 18*

Contents

SAFETY ADVICE
When you make any of the projects in this book, always put safety first. Be extremely careful with sharp scissors, needles, and pins and ask an adult if you need any help.

Learn stitches Page 30

Daisy button brooch Page 10

Dazzling Jewelry

Sparkling jewelry, made of beautiful gems and precious metals, can look like a stunning work of art. But there is a darker side to the production of jewelry, especially some of the industries that mine for metals, such as gold and platinum, or precious stones, such as rubies, emeralds, and diamonds.

Jewelry ethics

Mining for valuable materials used in jewelry all too often comes at a great cost to both the environment and the workers involved in their production. Environmental destruction through the use of dynamite and dangerous chemicals is still widespread. Workers are often expected to work in dangerous conditions, and child labor is commonplace in many cases.

Taking responsibility

There is a growing movement among jewelry designers to only use precious metals and stones obtained through responsible mining and healthy conditions for workers. They insist on being clear about their supply chains, demanding to know where and how their metals and stones have been obtained.

4

As well as being a great addition to your jewelry box, the crafts in this book make super presents!

All these fab crafts are made from stuff that usually gets thrown out!

Pretty, not precious

Beautiful jewelry can be made from all kinds of materials, not just precious metals and stones. And by choosing to avoid materials that can cause damage to the environment, you can be gorgeous and fashionable, but have a clear conscience too. Jewelry made from recycled materials is even better, transforming you into the Eco Queen of Bling!

Find your inner magpie

So what can you reclaim, reuse, and recycle to make the fabulous projects in this book? First of all, you need to find your inner magpie. Look at home, in thrift stores, and at rummage sales for anything shiny, sparkly, twinkly, and pretty. Sequins, buttons, and beads snipped off old clothes are great. Silky and shiny fabrics from old clothes, ties, and furnishing materials are ideal. Fastenings and catches from clothes and broken jewelry are essential. Reworking old, broken, or damaged pieces of jewelry is a must. Silk, satin, velvet, and sparkly ribbon, braid, and cords from packaging are always useful. And scrap paper in pretty colors and textures is endlessly versatile when it comes to designing and making your own dazzling jewelry.

Don't be trashy – recycle!

Charm bracelet

Create this personalized charm bracelet using small reclaimed objects such as beads, shells, pieces of broken jewelry, or an odd earring. Each object could have a special significance for you, helping to make this bracelet really special.

1 Assemble your charms and make sure they'll be easy to attach to the bracelet. If you like, you can paint some of the charms. To make sure the paint sticks well, mix a little PVA to the paint, then paint on and leave to dry.

2 Measure a length of ribbon or string around your wrist, making sure there's plenty of extra to tie the bracelet on, then snip it to the right length. Cut two more pieces of string or ribbon to the same length.

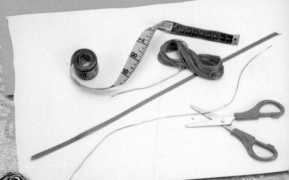

Recycling ribbons

You can find pretty ribbons in all kinds of places—from gift wrapping and chocolate boxes to packaging for cosmetics. Keep your eyes peeled and always save any scraps you find, so you've got a great selection to choose from!

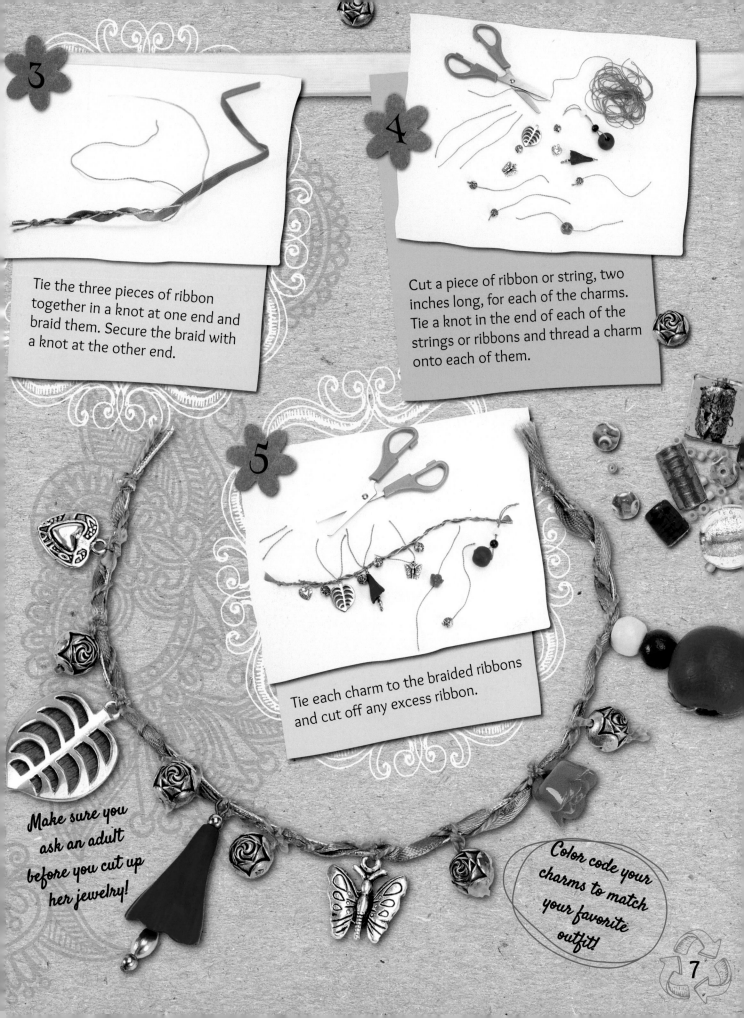

3

Tie the three pieces of ribbon together in a knot at one end and braid them. Secure the braid with a knot at the other end.

4

Cut a piece of ribbon or string, two inches long, for each of the charms. Tie a knot in the end of each of the strings or ribbons and thread a charm onto each of them.

5

Tie each charm to the braided ribbons and cut off any excess ribbon.

Make sure you ask an adult before you cut up her jewelry!

Color code your charms to match your favorite outfit!

Watch that bling!

Give an old watch a new lease on life by attaching a new, groovy, sparkling strap. To decorate, you can use sequins scavenged from old clothes.

1 Remove the strap from the watch. If you can't cut the straps off, check the box below for other ways of removing them.

2 Cut two lengths of ribbon that are each between 1.5 and 2 inches longer than one of the old straps.

3 Sew sequins onto the ribbons to decorate.

How to remove a watch strap

Most watch straps are attached to a little bar at the top and bottom of the watch face. Find the tiny hole in line with each bar. Press a needle or pin into the hole and it should release the bar. You may need to ask an adult to help you. Once the strap is off, slip the bar back into place. If you really can't get the strap off, visit your local jeweler and ask him if he can remove it. It should only take a second and he shouldn't need to charge you.

4

Loop one length of decorated ribbon through the bar at the top of the watch and sew on securely. Repeat with the second piece of ribbon at the bottom bar.

5

Cut the string into three pieces that are each 4 inches long. Tie a knot into one end of each of them. Thread beads onto each length of string.

6

You can sew sequins onto the ribbon to cover up any stitches.

Attatch the beads to the bottom bar of the watch and cut off any excess string.

9

Daisy button brooch

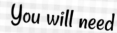
Create a beautiful floral brooch using an old tie, a button, and a brooch fastener. Ask for any old ties and search for the perfect button on old clothes. You may need to buy a brooch fastener, unless you can use one from a brooch you don't wear anymore.

2 Fold the tie up in an accordion shape, allowing about 4 inches for each fold.

1 Cut off the wider half of the tie and set it aside for another project; you only need the narrow end to make your brooch.

3 Pinch the center of the folded tie firmly between your thumb and forefinger and use your other hand to fan out the tie into a flower shape. Sew around the center a few times to keep it in place.

Sew the button into the center of the flower.

Sew the brooch fastener onto the back of the flower.

Button up!

Buttons are fantastic for upcycling. You can use them to make or decorate anything from jewelry and clothes to accessories and furnishings for the home.

How many ways can you think of to reuse a button?

Why not use your brooch to decorate your favorite hat?

11

Flutterby fascinator

Make a dazzling, fun fascinator by decorating an old hair comb with feathers, sequins, and stunning paper butterflies. Funky hair accessories are the latest trend so you'll be truly hip and happening with your hair swept back with this gorgeous hair comb.

1

Draw two butterfly shapes and a heart shape onto a piece of scrap paper. On a different colored piece of scrap paper, draw the same shapes, just smaller. Cut out all the shapes.

2

Cut three pieces of craft wire, each about 3 inches long. Stick the pieces of wire between the smaller butterfly or heart shapes and their larger equivalents.

Sourcing decorative paper

There are so many different places to find scrap paper that's just perfect for recycling into fab fashion statements. Save scraps of pretty wrapping and tissue paper from gifts and packaging. Tear out pages from magazines where you love the colors and designs. Also always keep decorative paper bags when you've been shopping.

3

Decorate the front top part of the hair comb with sequins.

4

Glue the wired shapes to the back of the comb, along with some feathers.

5

You can stick sequins to the shapes to add more sparkle!

In order to keep the feathers and wire in place, stick a length of ribbon across the back of the comb using craft glue.

Fabulous fluffy bangle

This beautiful bangle is the perfect way to use up scraps of fabric left over from sewing projects or reclaimed from old clothes. Choosing to wear jewelry made from fabric instead of precious metals and stones means you're lessening your personal impact on the environment.

1

Cut or rip the fabric into long, narrow strips. Don't worry about the strips being identical—this bangle looks better if there is a variety of fabric lengths and widths.

2

Wrap the embroidery thread around your wrist, then add about 4 inches to that length and snip. Tie a knot about 1 inch from one end and thread the other end into the needle.

Jewelry fastenings

Always save broken necklaces and bracelets, so that you can reuse the old parts. Hook and eye loops or pull-back catches are ideal for this bracelet, so just look through your collection of broken jewelry until you find one. Snip it off and make it into something new!

Roll each strip of fabric into a loose roll, with the pattern on the outside.

4

Thread each of the fabric rolls onto the embroidery thread.

5

tach the fastenings to the ends the thread with a double knot.

Why not make individual bangles for your best friends—they will adore them!

15

Sparkling choker

This necklace makes the ultimate style statement. Chokers just shout sophistication but are very simple to create. Look out for pretty ribbons on gift wrap, or maybe an old hair ribbon that would be just perfect. Snip the sequins off old clothes and look out for hooks and eyes on the waistband of an old skirt.

You will need

★ velvet ribbon
★ scissors
★ sequins
★ needle and thread
★ hooks and eyes

2

Decorate the ribbon with sequins in any design you like.

1

Measure the ribbon loosely around your neck, then snip to length.

3

Sew the hooks to one end and the eyes to the other.

Why not customize a party dress with sequins to match your choker?

Dazzling jewels!

Sequins are a great way to add sparkle without impacting the environment in the way that mining for precious stones such as diamonds can. Think about the kind of look you want to go for. You could sew a simple line of sequins along the center of the choker, or a line on each edge. You could make a pretty swirling pattern, or just go mad and cover the whole ribbon so it's sparkle, sparkle, sparkle all the way!

Pretty pendant

There's nothing worse than losing a favorite earring . . . but don't worry! Make this lovely pendant and you can still keep on enjoying your favorite pieces. A dangly earring will work best as you need something big and bold to make a real impact.

You will need

★ ribbon
★ single dangly earring
★ needle and thread
★ beads
★ scissors

1

Decide how low you want your pendant to hang, then cut the ribbon to length, allowing a little extra for tying the necklace on.

2

Thread the earring onto the ribbon.

No ribbon?

Can't find a piece of ribbon long enough? Never fear, you can use scrap fabric instead. Find some old clothes (checking first that you can use them) and cut out three long, narrow strips. Braid the strips together to make the cord for your necklace.

3 Cut three pieces of ribbon, all at different lengths. Tie a knot at one end of each piece of ribbon. Then use a needle to thread beads onto the ribbons.

4 Tie the ribbons to the pendant.

The earring we have used gives our pendant a lovely "vintage chic" look!

5 As a finishing touch, tie a length of ribbon around the top of the pendant in a pretty bow.

Button bracelet

Pretty buttons are great for turning into jewelry. Whether they're made from plastic, glass, mother of pearl, wood, or fabric, they're irresistible. When clothes are past their best, see whether you can rescue any buttons. A box of multicolored buttons is like a miniature treasure chest!

You will need

scissors

ribbon in different colors

lots of buttons

needle and thread

jewelry fastenings

1

Measure ribbon around your wrist and cut to length, allowing for a few inches extra at each end to attach the jewelry fastenings.

2

Look through your button collection and arrange your favorite ones in a row to create a pretty visual effect. You might like to layer them, placing small buttons on top of larger ones.

3

Using a needle and thread, sew together any layered buttons.

4

Attach the jewelry fastenings to the ends of the measured ribbon. You could add a pretty bow, too. You can attach it by sewing it to the ribbon.

There are countless different styles of buttons, so this little bracelet can be truly unique!

5

Attach the buttons to the ribbon using needle and thread.

Cell phone charm

Decorate your cell phone with its own personal jewelry! Make this accessory from homemade scrap paper beads or reuse beads from a broken necklace or bracelet.

You will need

- ★ colorful scrap paper
- ★ scissors
- ★ cocktail sticks or skewers
- ★ PVA glue
- ★ string or narrow elastic
- ★ needle

1 Cut the scrap paper into long, flared strips approximately 8 inches long, .5 inch wide at the top, 1 inch at the bottom.

2 Coat a strip of paper in a thin layer of glue, then wrap it around the cocktail stick, starting with the wider end of the strip. Repeat with the other strips of paper.

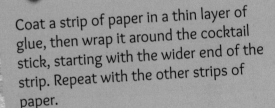

3

Leave the beads to dry slightly before gently sliding off the cocktail sticks. Leave them in a warm place to dry completely.

The art of rolling paper is called "quilling." People make the most amazing flowers using this method!

4

Knot the string or elastic at one end, then, using the needle, thread on the beads to a length of about 4 inches. Tie another knot to keep the beads in place, then tie a loop in the remaining string or elastic.

Upgrade?

Cell phones are made using rare and precious metals such as tungsten and cobalt. These metals can only be found in very few areas in the world and need to be mined. It's worth reconsidering upgrading your cell phone regularly to avoid the impact this has on the environment.

5

Attach the charm to your cell phone or cell phone cover using the loop.

Friendship anklet

You will need

★ scrap fabric, ribbon, or wool
★ darning needle
★ beads
★ scissors

This classic token of friendship is extra great when turned into an anklet rather than the more traditional bracelet. Make it special by making it from strips of fabric, ribbon, or wool and beads that have special significance—for example from a well-loved old top that's too old and shabby to wear, or a favorite necklace that's now broken.

1

Cut the ribbon, wool, or fabric strips into three pieces, each about 12 inches long.

2

Knot together the three lengths of your chosen material at one end and start braiding them. After every two or three loops, thread a bead onto one of the lengths.

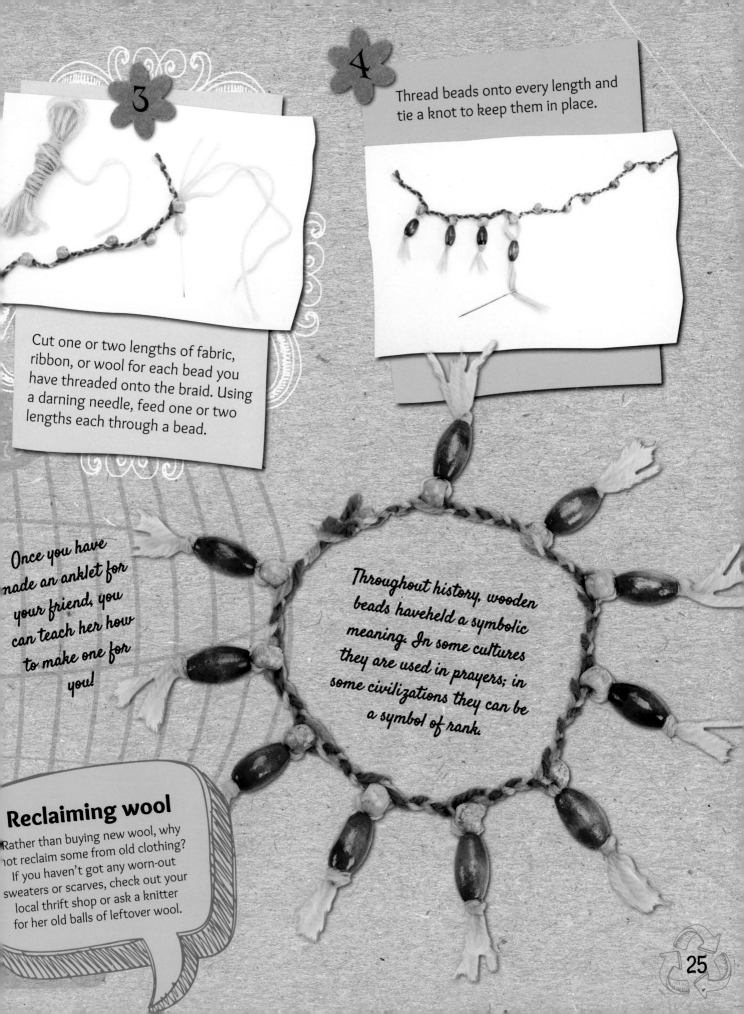

3

Cut one or two lengths of fabric, ribbon, or wool for each bead you have threaded onto the braid. Using a darning needle, feed one or two lengths each through a bead.

4

Thread beads onto every length and tie a knot to keep them in place.

Once you have made an anklet for your friend, you can teach her how to make one for you!

Throughout history, wooden beads have held a symbolic meaning. In some cultures they are used in prayers; in some civilizations they can be a symbol of rank.

Reclaiming wool

Rather than buying new wool, why not reclaim some from old clothing? If you haven't got any worn-out sweaters or scarves, check out your local thrift shop or ask a knitter for her old balls of leftover wool.

Not any old hair band

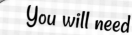

Transform an old hair band into a spectacular one by embellishing it with ribbons, sequins, and buttons—or whatever else takes your fancy! You won't need a tiara when you have this stunner tucked into your hair!

You will need

★ hair band
★ ribbon
★ scissors
★ foam sheets in different colors
★ buttons, beads, or sequins, to decorate
★ glue

1

Wrap a strip of ribbon or fabric around the hair band, securing it in place using glue.

2

Cut leaf and petal shapes out of the foam sheets.

3

Glue the foam sheet shapes together and decorate them with buttons, beads, or sequins.

4

Glue the flowers and leaves onto the hair band.

Did you know...
Mining waste is often dumped into the oceans, rivers, lakes, and streams, causing a threat to plant and animal life.

You can use any material that is sturdy and colorful to create these shapes.

Make a style statement!

Accessorizing with jewelry is one of the classic ways to really make a style statement. Whether you like it big and sparkly or subtle and subdued, the way you wear your jewelry says an awful lot about you!

Do you want to light up the room like a mirror ball or make an impression with a subdued outfit and single statement piece such as an outrageous fascinator? Do you like everything to have a bit of glitzy glamour, or do you like things cute and pretty? Are you a tomboy at heart who likes a bit of bling in the guise of a mobile charm, or are you the ultimate girly girl who wants sparkle, sparkle, sparkle?

Express yourself

Accessorize your look according to your mood. The joy of jewelry is that you can use it to express the inner you. And when you make it yourself, it has even more of a personal touch. Be flamboyant, be flirtatious, be pretty, be practical. Think about how you feel today, then raid your jewelry box and dare to express yourself.

Try out different looks and try out different pieces on different clothes. A brooch pinned to a plain black coat will look completely different on a floral dress, or fastened to a pretty cardigan. The same necklace and bracelet will look very different teamed with jeans and a sweater compared to how they look with a party dress on a special occasion.

It's all about you! This strap looks better than the ones you can buy, and it cost next to nothing. Best of all, it's unique!

Design your own

The only limits are your imagination . . . and the materials you can reclaim, recycle, and reuse!

nce you've mastered the basic ojects in this book, think about how u could reuse those skills to design ur own jewelry pieces. Create an nbellished necklace using the me skills used for the charm acelet on pages 6–7, or create howstopping hairpiece with loral theme using the same sic techniques used for the scinator on pages 12–13. ake a matching arm cuff to with the choker on pages –17, or make a beaded key g using the same skills used r the cell phone charm on ges 22–23.

Craft skills

How to thread a needle

Cut a length of thread. Make sure it is no longer than your arm; too long a piece of thread will become knotted and make sewing hard work. Pass the tip of the thread through the eye of the needle. If the ends are frayed, dampen them slightly. Hold the two ends of thread together and loop into a knot. Doubling up the thread will help to make your sewing stronger.

Starting and finishing a line of stitching

To start, fasten the thread to the fabric using a few backstitches. End a line of tacking with one backstitch or a knot.

Sewing on buttons

Buttons usually have two or four holes, or have a single loop underneath. They need to be sewn on very firmly with plenty of stitches as they are generally subject to lots of wear and tear.

For a two-hole or looped button, sew through the holes or loop onto the fabric about six times in the same direction. Tie off on the underside of the fabric.

For a four-hole button, use the same technique as for the two-hole button, using opposite holes to make a cross pattern.

Tacking stitch

This is used to hold the fabric in position while it is being permanently stitched and is ideal for gathering fabric into ruffles. Pass the needle in and out of the fabric in a line to make long, even stitches.

To make ruffles, do not tie off the line of stitching. Gently pull the thread, sliding the fabric together into gathers or ruffles. When you have created the desired effect, tie off with a backstitch or knot.

Running stitch

Similar to the tacking stitch, the running stitch uses smaller stitches. It is used for seams and for gathering and can also be used to decorative effect, particularly with wool or embroidery thread. You can stitch lines or curling patterns onto the surface of fabric.

Pass the needle in and out of the fabric in small, even stitches.

Whipstitch

This stitch is used to secure two pieces of fabric together at the edges.

Place two pieces of fabric on top of each other.
Fasten the thread to the inside of one piece of fabric. Pass the needle through both pieces of fabric from underneath, passing through where you have fastened the thread. Stitch through from the underside again to make a diagonal stitch about half an inch from the first stitch. Repeat.

Blanket stitch

This is a decorative stitch used to bind the edge of fabric. Use a contrasting colored thread for maximum effect.

Fasten the thread on the underside of the fabric, then pass the needle from the underside. Make a looped stitch over the edge of the fabric but before you pull it tight, pass the needle through the loop. Repeat.

Glossary

accessory: A fashion item such as jewelry, scarf, or bag that can be added to enhance your overall fashion look.

consumer: A person who buys products and services for personal use.

contaminant: A toxic or poisonous substance that infects or soils other substances.

eco: Often used in front of words to imply a positive effect on the environment, for example "eco-friendly" and "eco-fashion."

environment: The natural world, including air, soil, water, plants, and animals.

ethics: The standards of right and wrong; if something is unethical, it is deemed to be morally wrong or unacceptable.

landfill: Also known as a dump, a landfill is a site used for the disposal of waste materials.

mining: To dig coal, metal, precious stones, and other resources out of the ground.

recycle: To use something again, usually after processing or remaking in some way.

trend: Popular fashion or style at a given time.

toxic: Poisonous.

upcycle: To take something that is disposable and transform it into something of greater use and value.

Useful Web sites

freecycle.org: A Web site helping to keep unwanted consumer goods out of landfills. It brings together people who want to get rid of things and people who need those things.

etsy.com: A Web site where people can buy and sell handmade crafts. A great source for craft inspiration.

thriftyfun.com: A Web site where people can learn how to make handmade crafts.

Index

eco chic